CONSTRUCTION DEFECT CLAIMS/LITIGATION
A Two Case Study

Preface:

This eBook and the majority of material developed by me is from a personal and hands-on perspective, based on 40+ years of experience in the insurance claims industry. It is written in the first person narrative point of view and often relayed in a story format. I am passionate about the subjects presented and therefore you will read the word "I" quite often. In my desire to find the best method of presenting the information, I found that telling "my" story was the most efficient platform.

Hugh W. Black CPCU, ARM, AIC, CCLA

CONSTRUCTION DEFECT CLAIMS/LITIGATION
A Two Case Study

INTRODUCTION:

What is a Construction Defect Claim?

The California Supreme Court in the Montrose decision described it as a continuing or progressively deteriorating condition which causes injury or damage. The damage may not be discovered by the damaged party for days, months, or even years after it occurred.

Or:

Loss, injury, or deterioration, caused by the negligence, design, or accident of one person to another, in respect of the latter's person or property. (Source Black's Law Dictionary)

Most states or jurisdictions have a definition for CD claims either in their case law or by statute. In many states the definitions were developed in court decisions involving environmental or asbestos property damage or bodily injury litigation. They are sometimes called long tail exposures because the damage continues or progresses over a long period of time. These findings and definitions will be discussed in more detail on the Axiom website on a state by state basis.

CONSTRUCTION DEFECT CLAIMS/LITIGATION
A Two Case Study

OVERVIEW OF THE CD CLAIMS HANDLING PROCESS:

A Construction Defect Claim; (hereinafter referred to as CD Claim) usually arises out of large construction projects. But they can also involve one single family dwelling. The projects can be single family dwellings, condominiums, apartments, office buildings, commercial buildings, shopping centers, recreational developments or industrial developments. They can also be what is called mixed use developments which involve a combination of commercial and residential tenants or owners.

Multiple parties are typically involved in each CD claim which can include the plaintiff(s), developer, general contractor, construction manager, sub-contractors, material suppliers, manufacturers, and design professionals. One of the most complex cases I ever handled involved 80 subcontractors. It is not unusual for 20 to 30 sub-contractors and potentially material suppliers and other parties being involved in a single case.

Public entities and administrative agencies are normally not a party to the claim or lawsuit but they can or may have substantial influence on the outcome of the claim/litigation. Governmental immunity is usually a complete or partial bar to actively involving them in the claim or litigation.

Each of the parties referenced above will have one or more insurance companies which provided them insurance coverage over a period of time which can be as long as 10 to possibly 15 years. The majority of CD cases which are in litigation will last between two to eight years from the first report to resolution. Statutes of limitation can affect a number of issues including how long it will take to achieve a resolution. Consult with counsel and follow your company's policies and procedures regarding these issues.

Each of the insurance companies will have slightly different coverage and claim handling positions and approaches. Each of the parties will have different opinions regarding the scope of repair; method of repair; and the cost of the repairs. From an insurance company claims handling perspective there is the issue of different coverage positions regarding the damages or defects being claimed. Coordinating the number of parties that are involved usually results in a complex and difficult claim resolution process.

As an adjuster handling a CD claim it is important to always keep in mind that even if some or possibly all of the damages or defects being alleged may not be covered, the insured may be found legally liable for all of the damages or defects. This issue becomes important if the insured is still actively in business. Follow your company's policies and procedures.

Due to the number of parties typically involved in the CD claim or litigation it is extremely difficult to convince the plaintiff(s) and developer or general contractor to settle with the subcontractors and other parties separately. The number of parties complicates the settlement process. A settlement under these circumstances may require that you settle for a larger amount of money than your evaluation indicates to buy your peace.   Make sure you follow your company's policies and procedures in this regard.   Keep in mind that whatever amount you settle for may affect your CD claim settlements in future cases involving the same insured or trade.   The settlement amount you agree to in one case is like establishing a basement amount and the other parties will attempt to convince you over a series of cases to increase that amount. From a negotiation standpoint it is always, in my opinion, a good idea to put a lot of thought into how much you decide to offer given these circumstances. This can be extremely difficult when your litigation expenses are increasing.   I will discuss these issues and some possible strategies in more detail later in the book.

Each of the involved parties will have arguments regarding their respective liability positions.   I have been involved in several thousand CD claims over the last 30 years and they involved liability and damage disputes that were continually being argued among the parties over the life of the case.   This is not unusual in most type of claims but when you have 20 to 30 parties or more involved in the case it is extremely difficult for any particular party to reach a compromise or resolution.

The sheer number of parties involved contribute significantly to the complexity of the claim/litigation process and the difficulties that are encountered in attempting to resolve the claim(s) or litigation. For an adjuster a typical CD claim can involve a number of issues including coverage issues, additional insured issues, contractual liability issues, liability issues, damage issues, evaluation issues and resolution issues. Because of the difficulties that are encountered in CD claims and litigation including discovery issues a number of jurisdictions use mediators in an effort to reduce the overall cost involved in the process and to assist in the resolution of complex CD litigation. The mediators have been very successful in expediting the process and reducing the overall expenses. Could the process be improved? Of course there is always room for improvement.

When I first got involved in CD litigation 30+ years ago, mediators had not gotten involved in the California based resolution process. At that time it was a discovery nightmare with multiple parties propounding interrogatories, seeking document productions, participating in site inspections and taking multiple depositions. In addition there were constant battles over procedural issues. The courts were overwhelmed and no one understood CD cases and for that reason were not controlling the discovery process. At the time I described the process as a three ring circus. Actually it felt more like a 100 ring circus in some cases.

If there are multiple insurance companies for a particular insured the adjuster must attempt to gain the cooperation of the other adjusters to develop a plan of action to resolve the claim or litigation. This can be extremely difficult and frustrating and possibly even impossible without resorting to litigation between the insurance companies. In my opinion litigation should be a last resort in this situation and only after conducting a thorough cost-benefit analysis. Consult with counsel and follow your company's policies and procedures.

I am aware of a few situations where one or more insurance carriers have litigated coverage and possibly argued public policy issues with another insurance company. This is highly unusual and should be carefully and thoroughly discussed to consider the possible outcome and application of any judicial determinations on the handling of future CD claims before proceeding. I have seen a number of results that were, in my opinion, adverse to the insurance industry. Sometimes though you may not have any choice but to proceed with litigation under these circumstances. Discuss with consul, however, always follow your company's policies and procedures.

The majority of CD claims will already be in litigation when they are reported to your company. The exceptions usually involve either developers or general contractors almost exclusively. If the developer or general contractor has a Self-Insured Retention (SIR) the insurance company usually allows the insured to handle the claim and hopefully resolve it within the SIR. The SIR provisions in the insurance company policy may allow the insurance company to assume control over the handling of the CD claim. In my experience this does not happen very often. The amount of work that an adjuster would be required to do on a non-litigated CD claim usually prevents this approach. Consider your options carefully and follow your company's policies and procedures.

CONSTRUCTION DEFECT CLAIMS/LITIGATION
A Two Case Study

If the insurance company elects to handle a non-litigated CD claim it will require adherence to the appropriate state mandated Claims Settlement Practices statute if one exists. A number of states have enacted a Claims Settlement Practices statute. Follow the statute and your company's policies and procedures.

The Claim Settlement Practices statutes typically include the following provisions:

1. Prompt response to correspondence which calls for a response.

2. Misrepresentation of Policy Provisions

3. Prompt coverage decisions/Reservation of Rights/Non-Waiver

4. Prompt claim settlement or resolution

In my experience the majority of CD claims are litigated. There is a comfort level which is achieved when all of the involved parties reach a resolution which results in mutual releases, dismissals, and court approved settlements. For the lack of a better way to describe this type of resolution there are no loose ends to deal with when the claim is resolved. This type of resolution may not always be realistic or possible in certain claim situations. In my opinion there is something wrong with allowing a CD claim to go into litigation if it might possibly be prevented and hopefully controlled. In the event you do encounter this situation follow your company's policies and procedures.

CONSTRUCTION DEFECT CLAIMS/LITIGATION
A Two Case Study

I have been involved in several CD claims which, when reported, did not involve a lawsuit. The majority of them involved one single family home. I was able to work with the claimants and or their attorney to resolve the claim without resorting to litigation. The majority of these CD claims only involved two or three subcontractors and I was successful in gaining their cooperation in the mutual handling and resolution.

CONSTRUCTION DEFECT CLAIMS/LITIGATION
A Two Case Study

CASE NUMBER ONE

In the late 1990s I was handling CD claims for a particular insurance company. I was assigned a new CD claim involving a developer who had built 42 tract custom homes. The claim submission was in the form of a letter from the named insured's personal attorney. There was no reference in either the caption of the letter or in the body of the letter to any pending litigation. The letter indicated, among other things, that 12 of the homeowners were currently complaining about multiple construction defects and property damage allegedly due to the construction. Personal counsel anticipated additional homeowners would also be making claims shortly.

I obtained a copy of the insurance policy and verified that we had provided general liability coverage to the insured for the last five or six years and they were currently insured. I contacted the insured's personal counsel and confirmed there was no litigation currently pending. In fact none of the homeowners had retained counsel. Each of the houses had been sold for an amount slightly in excess of 1 million dollars. At that time no other parties had been placed on notice of the claims. Personal counsel assured me that the insured had subcontracted out all of the construction work to subcontractors.

Personal counsel for the insured inquired as to whether I wanted his law firm to handle the claim. I indicated to personal counsel that I would handle the claims myself. The insured did not have an SIR.

CONSTRUCTION DEFECT CLAIMS/LITIGATION
A Two Case Study

Personal counsel indicated to me that the insured was concerned about my handling the claims and not involving his law firm. I explained to personal counsel I had approximately 17 years of experience handling CD claims at that time. I issued a reservation of rights letter.

Over the next year personal counsel invited me to attend two meetings to discuss my handling and discuss the contents of the reservation of rights letter. In both meetings I was able to convince personal counsel that the homeowner claims were under control and were being resolved. I explained that the policy did contain a property damage deductible but we would not be seeking reimbursement until after the claims were resolved. Also we were not seeking any contribution from the insured for any non-covered property damage.

I was able to settle or resolve the claims for 33 of the 42 homeowners. Unfortunately two or three of the remaining nine homeowners were demanding significantly higher property damages than their homes had actually sustained. When we rejected their demands they retained counsel. Shortly after this occurred I left the company and the remaining nine homeowners decided to litigate their claims.

After my initial conversation with personal counsel for the insured I made several claim handling decisions:

1. The first issue involved whether to retain an attorney to handle the CD claims. I decided not to retain an attorney to handle the CD claims

because of the potential expense that would have been involved. I also did not want a potential dispute with personal counsel for the insured if the insurance company retained an attorney. Without any pending litigation there was no legal or contractual obligation to retain an attorney to represent the insured. I was also concerned that if an attorney became involved one or more of the homeowners might feel compelled to retain an attorney. If that occurred I knew this would likely result in the homeowner attorneys attempting to convince the remaining homeowners to retain them and the entire claim could end up in litigation which would increase the expenses and costs significantly. I also realized that the homeowner claims could result in litigation regardless of my efforts. I was willing to take that risk because there was no pending litigation.

2. The next issue involved whether to hire an independent adjuster to handle the CD claims. That would have been my first choice given my work load but unfortunately I was not aware of an independent adjuster who would have the time to effectively handle 42 complex non-litigated CD homeowner claims. I was also concerned about losing control of the claims handling process and one or more of the homeowners retaining counsel and the entire claim ending up in litigation. Effective communication is critical with independent adjusters, attorneys, experts and other parties. Without effective communication the

homeowner claims would have ended up in litigation. I will be discussing communication in my next book titled "Litigation Management".

3. The next issue to consider involved the nature and type of defects and damages that the homeowners were alleging. I was aware of some of the allegations but it was not clear what all of the defects and damages were for each of the homeowner claims based on the limited information we had received. It was obvious at the time that the only way to make that determination would involve having the homes inspected by a construction expert who could then provide me the information I needed to decide which subcontractors to involve in the CD claims handling and resolution process.

4. The next issue involved a decision whether to place all of the subcontractors involved in the original construction on notice of the claims and request their participation in the claim handling process. Personal counsel for the insured had assured me that the insured had signed contracts with each of the subcontractors who had been involved in the original construction. I requested copies of all of the contracts. Based on my experience I knew it would be extremely difficult to gain the cooperation of the subcontractors in the claim handling process since there was no pending litigation. I also knew it would take at least one year to get them actively involved. Also I knew there were no guarantees that any of them would willingly participate in the process and if they did there

would be numerous problems regarding the liability and damage issues. These potential issues based on my experience would result in the homeowners retaining counsel and litigating their claims. Since one of my main goals was to try to control expenses this would have reduced my ability to achieve that goal. Although there was no real conflict of interest in the event of litigation the insured may have attempted to retain independent counsel and we could have ended up in litigation regarding this issue.

After considering all of the issues discussed above I still had to decide what the most cost effective method or approach would be to handle the non-litigated homeowner CD claims. I decided that the most effective approach would be to utilize an experienced general contractor expert to meet with each of the homeowners to inspect, verify and document their various CD allegations and damages. Then work with the individual homeowners and the contractor of their choice to develop a scope of repair, method of repair, agree on the construction materials to be used and finally agree on a reasonable cost to complete those repairs. Then reach a settlement with each of the individual homeowners.

Another consideration was to involve the subcontractors in the resolution process and when. There are several different approaches that can be utilized to involve the subcontractors. Any approach would require that the general contractor expert thoroughly document the defects and damage for each of the homeowner claims sufficiently to pursue the subcontractors in a breach of contract and negligence action or possibly an arbitration. I personally don't favor arbitration but this type of claim resolution might be the best approach to achieve a reasonable resolution with a minimum amount of expense and costs. This can be accomplished by utilizing a combination of repair estimates, photographs and possibly videotaped documentation both prior to the repairs and during the repairs. Also the testimony of the general contractor expert in any legal action would be crucial to achieve a reasonable recovery from the subcontractors, material suppliers and product manufacturers.

There was also the possibility of design errors. At the time I decided to wait until after the inspections of the homes and discuss the possibility with the general contractor expert. If there was an issue in this regard I would decide how to proceed depending on several factors which could possibly include whether the insured had contracted with the design professionals. Or the design professionals were employees of the insured. As there were no design issues it did not become a factor.

I was not familiar with any general contractor experts in the area where the housing tract was located. I called several defense attorneys in the area asking for a referral. One of the defense attorneys referred me to a general contractor expert who he had used in the past. He suggested that particular general contractor expert and indicated that he had over 20 years of actual general contracting experience and had been working as a forensic construction expert for a number of years.

I contacted the general contractor expert and confirmed he had over 25 years of actual general contractor experience in addition to having testified in a number of depositions and in several trials involving CD defect and damage issues. We discussed my claims handling philosophy. As a result of our conversation I was confident of his ability to assist me in the approach I wanted to take and his ability to help me in achieving my claim resolution goals.

I selected a defense attorney to retain in the event that the claims became litigated. I contacted the defense attorney and explained the approach I was going to pursue. I requested that he open a legal file to protect the general contractor's activities during the inspection process and his efforts to resolve the individual homeowner claims under the attorney-work product privilege. I also indicated to defense counsel that his services would be needed to finalize the settlements with the individual homeowners and in the event the claims became litigated to defend the named insured. Defense counsel agreed to my approach.

I re-contacted the general contractor expert and we agreed on the following plan of action:

1. I explained to the general contractor expert that he would be meeting with each of the 42 homeowners individually and documenting their defect and damage allegations. The inspection would also include personally obtaining

photographic evidence of the alleged defects and damages.

2. I then wanted him to work with each of the homeowners to select a contractor of their choice to provide us with a repair estimate.

3. The general contractor expert and I agreed that he would have a list of five general contractors available for the homeowners to select from to develop their repair estimate if they did not have one they wanted to use. The general contractor expert told me that during the inspection process five of the homeowners selected one of the general contractor experts on the list but the remainder utilized their own general contractor.

4. The general contractor expert would review each of the repair estimates and work with the contractors and the homeowners to reach a mutually agreeable scope of repair, method of repair and cost of repair for each home. This would also include an agreement on the construction materials to be utilized in the repair process.

5. As part of the settlement process the general contractor expert would obtain permission from the homeowner to videotape the individual home repairs for a subsequent recovery action against any negligent or contractually liable parties.

6. I told the general contractor expert he might have to sit in on any settlement discussions in a contract action to assist if there were any issues regarding the repairs.

7. The general contractor expert and I would discuss the need for his inspections of the home repairs as they occurred.

After our discussion I was convinced the general contractor expert would be able to follow my plan of action and he agreed to take on the assignment. I then re-contacted the defense attorney who had made the referral and provided him the details regarding my plan of action. Involving counsel early in the process gave him more flexibility regarding the potential production of evidence gathered during the inspection and repair process in a subsequent legal action. Utilizing this approach allowed me the flexibility to utilize counsel on an as needed basis to prepare for a possible contract action.

I then re-contacted the general contractor expert and gave him permission to begin contacting the individual homeowners. I emailed the homeowner correspondence and the documentation provided to me by personal counsel for the insured to the general contractor expert.

Over the next eight months the general contractor expert followed my instructions with the following results:

1. He inspected all 42 homes and documented the alleged defects and property damage.

2. All but nine of the homeowners agreed to hire their own contractor to provide repair estimates.

3. The repair estimates ranged from a minimum of $3,500 for three of the houses to a high of $101,000 for one of the houses. The remainder of the 33 home repair estimates fell between these two dollar amounts. Several of them were $85,000 for each house. The average cost of repair for all 33 homes was $46,000.

4. One of the homeowners indicated that she had no damage but I decided to pay her $3,500 to obtain a release for precautionary reasons. I was concerned that she might be persuaded to join with the nine homeowners who had decided to retain counsel.

5. One of the nine homeowners demanded $250,000 even though her property damage was approximately $135,000. The other eight homeowners decided they did not want to participate in the inspection process and decided to retain counsel.

A number of states; 31 based on my research have enacted "Right to Repair" statutes which allows the developer or general contractor under certain circumstances the opportunity to repair or pay for the repairs to the homes they built before the homeowners can file a lawsuit. Each statute is different and the right is not absolute. Be sure you follow your company's policies and procedures if you decide to proceed within the provisions of your local statute. We will be providing information as we obtain it regarding these statutes on our website. As of the writing of this book the website is under construction.

When the general contractor expert had analyzed the repair estimates developer by the contractor for the homeowner and they agreed on the cost of repair he submitted the documentation to me for review and approval. I requested settlement authority and once received I instructed defense counsel to meet with the homeowner to go over the settlement figures and secure a general release. As indicated above this approach worked for 33 of the 42 homes in the construction project.

I paid the general contractor expert $25,000 for the assignment. I don't recall how much I paid defense counsel to meet with each of the homeowners and secure the signed releases.

Just prior to finishing the process I left the insurance company. I stayed in contact with the general contractor expert and used him on other CD and General Liability claims. He has told me that he talked to other parties in the subsequent litigation and provided me the following information:

1. Nine of the 42 homes did end up in litigation.

2. The litigation lasted four years.

3. The settlement for each house was approximately $285,000. The total settlement for all nine homes would have been approximately $2,565,000.

4. In typical CD litigation all of the subcontractors who had any potential liability exposure would have participated and probably participate in the

settlement. The subcontractors should have paid the majority of the settlements.

5. According to the general contractor expert there were four separate inspections and probably destructive testing during the litigation at each of the nine homes.

As I was no longer at the insurance company I do not know how much they paid in litigation expenses to include defense counsel, experts and other expenses. Based on my experience the legal and expert expenses incurred by the insurance company were probably somewhere between $500,000 and $750,000 over the four years. This is only an estimate on my part. A significant portion of this amount was probably paid by the subcontractors and their insurance companies based on an indemnity obligation contained in the construction contracts and or an additional insured defense obligation.

I don't know if the insurance company filed a separate indemnity action against the subcontractors or attempted to recover the settlements with the 33 homeowners in a cross complaint. Each CD case is different but since the insured subcontracted out all of the construction work and if the insurance company followed through with documenting the homeowner repairs they should have had an excellent chance of recovering close to 100% of the settlements.

In my opinion it is possible to effectively handle a non-litigated CD claim and control the expenses, settlements and other issues. It requires a plan of action, effective communication and the realization that everything may not proceed as you initially planned. This approach should be considered. Be sure to align any action you undertake with your company's policies and procedures.

If a CD claim is in litigation it is possible in some cases for the insurance carrier(s), the developer, or general contractor, to attempt to expedite the settlement or resolution process. Unfortunately it is more difficult than for non-litigated CD claims. It is very difficult but not impossible for a subcontractor to have any control or influence over the handling, resolution process or settlement of a CD claim in litigation. I will be discussing different approaches on our website.

CONSTRUCTION DEFECT CLAIMS/LITIGATION
A Two Case Study

CASE NUMBER TWO

In 1985 or 1986 I was assigned several CD cases in litigation involving condominium complexes. My insured was a developer in one of the CD cases that I was assigned. I confirmed coverage and sent out a reservation of rights letter. I retained defense counsel from the company's approved list of attorneys. I had just started at that particular company and was not familiar with the attorneys on the approved list. At that time there was very little case law and no statutes that specifically involved the handling of CD claims.

I contacted defense counsel and discussed how to approach the handling considering the fact there was very little legal guidance regarding CD claims. Defense counsel indicated that he had dealt with the plaintiff attorney who was involved in the condominium case in the past on several other cases. He convinced me that he had developed a rapport with the plaintiff attorney and was confident that we could expedite the claims handling, discovery process and resolution. Hopefully in the process control the overall expenses.

Defense counsel and I discussed and agreed on the following plan of action:

1. Plaintiff counsel had provided a defect list and information regarding the defects and property damage which were being alleged. The alleged defects and property damage involved the structures and common areas controlled by the homeowners association. We confirmed with plaintiff counsel that none of the individual

condominium owners had any defects or had any property damage. For these reasons defense counsel and I agreed to concentrate our efforts on the alleged claims being made by the homeowners association. If the individual condominium owners made claims at a later date we would deal with them on an as needed basis.

2. Defense counsel was successful in convincing plaintiff counsel to work with us in an effort to resolve the litigation without engaging in extensive litigation. We agreed on a timetable to begin and a projected completion date for the process.

3. As part of the agreement we agreed with plaintiff counsel to limit legal discovery to exchange only the information that would be necessary to accomplish our plan of action. This involved some document production, limited interrogatories and no depositions. We all agreed that additional discovery including depositions would only be necessary if our plan of action was not productive.

4. Defense counsel and I also agreed to hold off in filing and serving cross complaints on the subcontractors until we had some additional information. Hopefully at that time we would be better informed about which subcontractors to involve in the plan of action and the litigation.

5. The plan of action we all agreed upon involved both sides selecting experts to inspect the condominium complex to identify the alleged

defects and property damage. Then all of the experts would meet to discuss their findings and agree on the defects and property damage. The experts would then work together to develop a joint scope of repair and a method of repair. Then both sides would utilize their own cost estimator to develop a cost of repair for both the structures and the common areas. We would then complete a bid comparison and work out any differences if necessary.

6. Defense counsel proceeded to obtain the documents we needed. I don't recall if he propounded any interrogatories but if so it did not take very long to receive the plaintiff's answers and the information we needed. My experience is that cooperation can be infectious.

7. Defense counsel forwarded me the construction contracts for the various subcontractors who had worked on the project. The insured had subbed out all of the work except for general cleanup of the construction site. I read all of the subcontracts and determined the scope of work for each of the subcontractors. Defense counsel and I compared notes and agreed on the work completed by each of the subcontractors.

8. Defense counsel and I then went over the alleged defect list and property damage together. We both identified the five subcontractors who had the majority of the potential liability for the alleged defects and property damage. I instructed defense counsel

to file but not serve the cross complaint on the subcontractors.

9. I then instructed defense counsel to place the five subcontractors we identified on notice of the pending litigation. I suggested that he include a copy of the un-served cross complaint and a copy of the construction subcontracts along with the plaintiff's list of defects and property damage. In the notice letter he invited each of the subcontractors to join with us in the plan of action to resolve the litigation. The notice letter also indicated that we were going to proceed with or without their involvement and included the timetable we had agreed upon with plaintiff counsel. I considered whether to place the subcontractors on notice myself but decided that it would be more persuasive if defense counsel sent the notices.

10. Defense counsel and I agreed not to involve the few remaining subcontractors whose potential exposure was extremely minimal. We both agreed that the more parties that we got involved in the process the more potential for problems and the possibility the situation could end up in protracted litigation. Prior to this case I had not been involved in this type of approach so there was some risk involved. But when I considered the potential for a much more reasonable settlement and overall reduced expenses I felt it was worth the risk. Fortunately my settlement authority at that particular company, although not unlimited, allowed me to make the decisions that needed

to be made to pursue the plan of action. Follow your own company's policies and procedures.

11. According to the timetable all of the experts met at the condominium complex and conducted a joint inspection. Interestingly all of the five subcontractors sent experts to observe the joint inspection and they later attended and participated in the discussions regarding the identity of the defects and property damage. They also participated in the development of the scope of repair and method of repair.

12. It took several months of concerted effort to get all of the experts to agree on the defects and property damage and allocation of damages to the appropriate subcontractors. Then to agree on a scope of repair and method of repair. To be honest I was amazed at the amount of time it took to achieve it considering the number of involved parties. I was convinced that at any time that we would not be able to reach an agreement with the plaintiff and we would end up in expensive litigation. But I also knew that with the efforts we had completed to that point we would be much further ahead towards resolving the litigation than if we had not made the attempt. Both sides including the plaintiff were taking a chance and, in my opinion, the only thing we had to rely on was our mutual trust of each other and the desire to reach an amicable resolution.

13. Both sides then hired cost estimators to price out the scope and method of repair. To say I was a little nervous during this stage would be

an understatement. We were so close to reaching a settlement.

14. After the repair estimates were completed and exchanged both sides completed a bid comparison. When I received the bid comparison I was very surprised. The difference between the two repair estimates after adjustments was only slightly in excess of $15,000 considering that the total repairs were in the area of $250,000.

15. After a brief discussion with plaintiff counsel we agreed to split the difference. I believe in the actual split we agreed to pay 60% of the difference between the two repair estimates.

16. After some persuasion we were able to convince the insurance carriers for the five subcontractors to contribute 85% of the final agreed upon repair costs. I decided not to pursue the remaining subcontractors as it would not have been cost effective. The entire process took approximately six months. Releases, dismissals and good faith settlements were obtained.

A month or so later I received another lawsuit involving the same plaintiff attorney which again involved a condominium complex. I contacted the same defense attorney to repeat the process. Unfortunately shortly after we began the process defense counsel received an appointment to the municipal court bench which he accepted. Shortly after that I transferred to another office with the same company and was no longer involved in the handling of that claim. Later I spoke to someone at my prior office and learned that shortly after I left plaintiff counsel decided to abandon the plan of action we had pursued in the first case and the second case proceeded though the normal litigation process.

In my experience the types of claims handling approaches discussed in Case Number One and Case Number Two can only be attempted by the insurance carrier(s) for the developer or general contractor. There are benefits and potential drawbacks to the approaches. You have much better control over the entire claims process. There is a real potential for the insurance carrier(s) for the developer or general contractor to reduce the amount of their expenses, costs and loss payments. The other potential is that you may not be able to recover 100% of your loss payments. It will be impossible with any degree of certainty to predict the amount of your potential recovery. Based on my experience it will probably be worth it based on the expenses that would be saved whether the claim is litigated or not. It also requires the claims person to have enough confidence in their ability to control and direct the handling of the claim(s) to be successful.

The keys to success:

1. Follow your company's policies and procedures.
2. Confirm coverage and depending on your state and jurisdiction place the appropriate insurance carriers for the insured on notice. I will be

discussing coverage triggers and allocation of damages in this book and on the website.

3. If there are other potential carriers who may have coverage it could be difficult to convince them to participate in the process. If they refuse to participate you will have to decide whether to proceed and then pursue them later. Discuss this issue with counsel.

4. The ability to effectively document the defects and property damage during the handling of the claim. If the claim is not in litigation document the actual repairs after the settlement which will significantly increase the potential for a substantial recovery from other negligent parties.

5. Communicating effectively with counsel, experts, and other claims handling personnel regarding the goals and the plan of action to achieve those goals. This is crucial to achieve success. I cover communication in my next book "Litigation Management".

6. Making an informed decision as to when and which parties need to be placed on notice and the best approach to gaining their involvement, cooperation and participation in the resolution of the claim.

7. Working with the other parties whether they are subcontractors, material supplier, manufacturers, or other possibly negligent parties to achieve your goals and a resolution of the claim.

8. Work with counsel and follow your company's policies and procedures to determine if a contribution and or contract action would be appropriate.   This will require a cost-benefit analysis.

9. If you are successful in following the plan of action and gain the cooperation of the other parties it may be possible to achieve the same results.   Be careful about deciding to create a handling model to follow because no two claims are exactly the same.

As I indicated earlier in the book it is extremely difficult for an insurance carrier for a subcontractor to attempt the same approach as discussed above. I have been successful on several claims but there are only certain circumstances that may be appropriate to consider the approaches.   I have included one such claim on the Axiom website.   (www.axiomclaimsanakytics.com) It required the use of independent counsel to be successful.

CD CLAIMS HANDLING

Handling and resolving CD claims can be a complex process which is complicated by the unique issues involved. One home office claims supervisor described CD claims handling as being "abstract". There are a number of dictionary definitions for the word "abstract". I usually describe CD claims handling as starting off utilizing normal or the usual claims handling approaches. But at a certain point it can become very difficult to reach a final resolution because of the number of parties involved in the process. This can be frustrating but I have found that patience is the key to surviving the process. I hope this book will assist you to better understand the process.

Like most casualty insurance claims it is impossible to provide a specific order of handling steps to follow. They usually start off easy but quickly develop into a complex process where the different issues such as coverage, investigation, evaluation and resolution often overlap and it can become difficult to obtain the information you need to properly evaluate the claim or claims. Because there are typically multiple parties involved in the CD claims handling process these problems can be overwhelming if you are not organized and are not familiar with the unique aspects involved in the process.

My goal is to try and provide you with some insights into how to handle and resolve CD claims based on my 40+ years of experience.

CONSTRUCTION DEFECT CLAIMS/LITIGATION
A Two Case Study

COVERAGE ISSUES

I cannot provide you with a magical formula to use in resolving CD claims as like other claims each of them are unique. The best advice I can give you is to study the principles; ask questions when in doubt; and follow your company's policies and procedures. It is extremely critical that you identify the issues raised by each claim and work towards resolving them.

CD claims are a type of General Liability claim that have unique coverage issues which affect indemnity and the duty to defend. Different fact situations require different interpretations and application of the policy provisions. For example each state has a slightly different coverage trigger which can result in different allocation issues. Coverage endorsements can affect the application of coverage. With multiple parties involved in the CD claim handling and resolution process a thorough investigation and analysis is critical to avoid potential problems. Follow your company's policies and procedures.

Insurance Underwriters can and will draft policy language that can be difficult to interpret. At one insurance company I was reading a Commercial General Liability Policy which appeared to have typical language except for one paragraph. The policy had been written as an occurrence policy for a large building developer. I read the unusual paragraph over several times trying to figure out how it would apply. I eventually realized that the underwriter was attempting to convert the occurrence form to a claims made coverage form using only the language in that paragraph. I discussed the language in the paragraph with the underwriter who confirmed that was his intent.

The majority of the policy forms I have dealt with were published by the Insurance Service Office (ISO). I have seen some forms from AAIS which is another rating bureau which also publishes policy forms for their clients to utilize in their policies. All policy language needs to be thoroughly read and compared to the facts of the claim being handled to avoid potential problems.

There are other rating bureaus which publish policy forms for their clients to use which I have encountered on a number of claims. If you typically use ISO policy forms and you receive a policy form published by one of the other rating bureaus it can be like learning how to interpret coverage all over again. Not only do you have to read the policy language very carefully but then compare the facts of the CD claim to that language to determine if there is a potential for coverage and to what extent. I have several cases where a policy contained ISO policy forms but it also contained policy forms from other sources and also manuscript policy language. It is imperative that you carefully compare the policy language to make sure there is no conflicting language that could affect coverage.

Insurance underwriters will draft manuscript policies and endorsements. In some cases an attorney or broker may have been involved in the drafting process. If an attorney and or underwriter drafted the policy or more likely an endorsement you will have to discuss the intent of the policy language with that individual if possible. On one case I was not allowed access to the underwriter. If possible I will question the attorney or underwriter regarding the origin of the language and the purpose and intent of the policy language. Drafting policy language is extremely difficult based on my experience because it is almost impossible to foresee the various claim situations to which it may potentially have to be applied.

On larger risks the broker for the insured may be involved. These types of policies typically require extensive analysis. Often the language is negotiated between underwriting and the insured. Unfortunately the claims department is not always consulted prior to drafting the policy language which can result in difficult claims handling situations. If this is the situation consult with the underwriter and the broker, if involved, in the policy drafting process, to assist in determining the intent of the parties as it relates to the CD claim you are currently handling. The policy language in this situation has probably not been litigated and may require extensive negotiations with the underwriter, the insured, and possibly the broker to achieve an amicable resolution if a dispute arises. Effective communication with the parties involved in the drafting process will hopefully result in a resolution and the avoidance of litigation. Coverage counsel may be of some benefit in this situation. Follow your company's policies and procedures.

Most policy forms contain a form number and an effective date. A few endorsements and policy forms do not include a form number or date. I was never able to determine the publisher or origin of the policy forms that were involved. This problem can result in some very unique coverage situations that may require coverage counsel to assist you in your analysis. Try to analyze the policy form yourself initially and follow your company's policies and procedures.

Insurance policy interpretation is a vital and interesting process. As there are literally hundreds and possibly thousands of different General Liability policy forms and no two CD claims are exactly the same it is impractical for me to attempt to provide you with any significant guidance in this area in this book. Follow your company's policies and procedures in this regard.

As part of this book I have included a document from a coverage attorney I have used for CD claims. The document provides some guidelines and guidance for coverage situations and reservation of rights letters that are unique to CD claims but could provide some guidance for other GL claims. My experience has been that most insurance claims departments utilize form reservation of rights letter that are tailored to consider the facts and specific coverage issues unique to the claim that is the subject of the reservations. Coverage counsel is sometimes used to write reservation of rights letters. (See Appendix A)

I have attached a relatively complex reservation of rights letter that I authored several years ago. At the time I was working at a third party administrator handling CD claims and Professional Liability claims. I was assigned a complex CD claim that involved two separate CD claims which were both in litigation. The two lawsuits both involved homes in the same construction project. At the time the two lawsuits had not been consolidated but a reservation of rights letter needed to be sent to the named insured. The client insurance company retained coverage counsel. The coverage attorney contacted me and asked me to write the reservation of rights letter. He instructed me to include the reservations for both lawsuits in one letter.

I proceeded to write the 27 page reservation of rights letter and emailed it to coverage counsel to review and let me know whether to send it to the named insured. The coverage attorney asked me to change two words and eliminate one sentence and mail it to the named insured. This particular reservation of rights letter was written to reserve the insurance company's rights on two separate lawsuits based on the facts and coverage issues related to only those two lawsuits. The letter is not a template to be used for every reservation of rights letter. Follow your company's policies and procedures as it relates to the need for a reservation of rights and the language and format to be used. (See Appendix B)

DOCTRINE OF REASONABLE EXPECTATIONS

Generally speaking the application of this doctrine by a court to a specific claim and set of facts can result in an extension or broadening of coverage to an insured where there does not appear to be any insurance coverage available based on your investigation. The doctrine is sometimes referred to as the insured's ability to receive the "benefit of the bargain". This has been interpreted by the courts to mean that the insured paid their premium and that they expected to receive certain coverage in return.

Will the insured be able to convince a jury there is some merit to this argument? If the insured is successful the result could alter, broaden or change the coverage provided to the insured. It is an argument that is raised sometimes where there is a dispute regarding the availability of coverage and the duty to defend.

Consult with counsel and consider your company's policies and procedures regarding this issue. I have found that asking counsel good questions in this situation can be beneficial. Then follow your company's policies and procedures.

One court which found coverage, which had been in dispute, suggested the following issues to consider when evaluating the possibility that the doctrine might be applied:

1. the actual policy provisions;

2. the presence of any ambiguity;

3. language which serves as a hidden exclusion;

4. oral communication from the insurer explaining key but vague conditions or exclusions; and

5. whether the policy provision is known to the public generally

In my opinion you should keep this doctrine in mind when evaluating coverage. It may become a factor in your coverage considerations and claim evaluation. It always bothered me when someone made this argument when it did not appear to apply. Unfortunately the final decision maker in this regard would be a judge and jury who may be more lenient in granting coverage to an insured. This doctrine should be considered during every aspect of the claims handling process to avoid potential problems, in my opinion. Almost every state has considered this argument.

Additional Material
At my request, Jim McFaul a coverage attorney who I have collaborated with in the past, agreed to write an educational paper regarding the need for and the use of reservation of rights letters. I specifically requested that he write a general analysis which would have application to most states.
Hugh W. Black CPCU, ARM, AIC, CCLA

Appendix A

RESERVING RIGHTS IN CONSTRUCTION DEFECT
LITIGATION

When an insurer undertakes to defend one of its insureds sued for damages in a construction defect case, a critical initial step is to thoroughly examine the claims advanced in the suit in light of the coverage the insurer provides, and, unless all claims advanced in the suit are clearly covered (which is rare), reserve the right to deny indemnity for the claims which are not covered. Under the terms of the commercial general liability (CGL) coverage available in today's insurance marketplace, it is an undeniable fact that the vast majority of the damage claims at issue in construction defect litigation are simply not covered. Every lawyer and insurance claims professional engaged in construction defect litigation knows that insurers pay to settle CD lawsuits primarily because they must otherwise pay to *defend* them. Because CGL insurers bear the burden of defending their insureds in any suit where there is at least the possibility or potential for covered damages, and because construction defect suits usually do include at least some covered claims, the insurer is on the hook. And because the expense of defending construction defect suits is extraordinarily high, insurers in most cases will prefer to settle rather than go to trial, and the settlement will usually reflect an assessment of the insured's liability exposure (i.e., whether the insured is actually responsible for the alleged defects, and what it will cost to repair them).

Whether the claims are actually *covered* under the insurer's policy is, very often, completely disregarded, even by the insurer paying the claim, given that the economics of CD litigation usually favor settlement over trial.

Why should an insurer reserve rights? Since the overwhelming majority of construction defect cases settle short of trial, it is a fair question whether there is any reason for the insurer to bother reserving rights. The answer is simple. Since at least some cases do *not* settle, the insurer will lose its right to challenge its obligation to pay a judgment against its insured, covered or not, if it defended the insured without a reservation of rights. And even in cases which do settle, a well-drafted reservation of rights letter and an insurer willing to aggressively inject its coverage position into the settlement dynamic will often improve the insurer's bottom line.

Here is why the reservation of rights letter is necessary for the insurer to preserve its coverage position. Under principles of contract law, one party to a contract can lose its rights vis-à-vis the other party if it knowingly and voluntarily "waives" them. Under a doctrine with similar effect known as "estoppel," Party A to a contract may be precluded (or "estopped"), from asserting its rights as against Party B, if Party A does or fails to do something which causes Party B to reasonably believe those rights will not be asserted.

The doctrines of waiver and estoppel also apply to *insurance* contracts, and each has been applied the preservation (or loss) of an insurer's coverage defenses. An insurance company which undertakes to provide a defense to its insured without adequately advising its insured that it is reserving its rights, can, in some jurisdictions, be found to have "waived" its right to later challenge coverage for a claim. In other jurisdictions, a court may determine that an insurer is "estopped" to disclaim coverage, as a result of undertaking an insured's defense without a reservation of rights, if the insured was misled into believing there was no problem with the availability of coverage for any ultimate judgment.

When should an insurer reserve rights? Like the old joke about voting in Chicago, an insurer should reserve rights "early and often." By issuing a reservation of rights at the same time it assumes its insured's defense, an insurer effectively precludes any argument that it has "waived" its right to disclaim coverage (in waiver jurisdictions), and (in estoppel jurisdictions), effectively eliminates the insured's ability to assert that it relied, to its detriment, upon the apparent *absence* of coverage defenses.

While the case law varies throughout the United States, it is correct to say that there is a direct correlation between the length of an insurer's delay, and the risk that the insurer will lose its coverage defenses. Some jurisdictions have been known to impose what insurers believe to be very harsh results, finding a waiver of coverage defenses based upon even a brief assumption of the insured's defense without asserting a reservation of rights. By contrast, other jurisdictions, principally those which apply estoppel principles to the loss of coverage defenses, have permitted insurers to retain their coverage defenses even after assuming an insured's defense for some period of time, even a year or more in some cases, at least in the absence of actual harm to the insured due to the delay.

For obvious reasons, the rule of thumb should *always* be to issue a reservation of rights as early as possible. And if grounds for reserving rights are not apparent at the outset of a suit, rights should be reserved as promptly as possible once the need to reserve rights becomes apparent.

In addition to reserving "early," an insurer should reserve "often." Despite some popular belief to the contrary, an insurer's assertion of its reservation of rights should not be thought of as a "one-off" event, to be issued at the beginning of the case and then forgotten about. Particularly in more serious cases, and especially as any serious case approaches trial, the insurer should actively communicate with its insured, either directly or through coverage counsel, regarding the problems with coverage. Not only does this approach serve to protect the insurer from losing its coverage defenses; it is actually favorable to the *insured's* interests. While no insured is excited to hear that its coverage is or may be unavailable, an open dialog between the insurer and insured at least avoids unpleasant, last-minute surprises at mediations, settlement conferences or trial. Beyond that, and at least with insureds with considerable means, the insurer's polite but direct advocacy of its own coverage position during the litigation of a CD case can, and regularly does, achieve the direct benefit of a contribution from the insured toward settlement.

How should an insurer reserve rights? In order to be effective, of course, an insurer wishing to reserve rights in assuming an insured's defense must advise its insured of the problems with coverage clearly, and *in writing*.

No one would dispute the fact that reservation of rights letters are deadly-boring. In their typical form, they are overlong, full of extensive quotations of insuring agreements, policy exclusions and conditions (much of which is unnecessary), and typically employ legal terms which the ordinary policyholder finds completely opaque. That's true. No more mind-numbing, however, than the average new car purchase contract, or the endless terms and conditions people scroll through at high speed, without reading, when joining iTunes. A properly prepared and issued reservation of rights will have its desired effect regardless of whether the insured understands it, or even reads it.

For a letter which is rarely read, from front to back, by its intended recipient, however, the content of the reservation of rights letter is very important. Most claims personnel and insurance coverage counsel have had the anxiety-inducing experience of being on the eve of trial, in trial, or staring at a verdict post-trial, and digging a reservation of rights letter out of the claims file years after it was written, looking to see if rights regarding that key policy exclusion were, or were not, reserved.

When it comes to the "how" of drafting reservation of rights letters, the insurer should be very careful to (1) consider all facts pertaining to the claims asserted against the insured, both as they may be pled in any complaint, along with facts known to the insurer from any source, and (2) give consideration to how the coverage available under the insurer's policy applies to those claims, and reserve rights on all potentially available bases. When in doubt as to whether a particular policy exclusion or other coverage defense may apply, the insurer generally *should* (except as considerations discussed immediately below may dictate otherwise), reserve rights on that exclusion or coverage defense.

Are there consequences to reserving rights on particular grounds? The answer to this question, in most jurisdictions, is yes. If an insurer reserves its rights with respect to a coverage defense which depends upon facts which themselves are "in issue" in the lawsuit the insurer is defending, and which defense counsel might be in position to influence, many states provide that the insurer must allow its insured to select defense counsel.

CONSTRUCTION DEFECT CLAIMS/LITIGATION
A Two Case Study

Much has been written about the so-called tripartite relationship between the insurer, its insured and defense counsel. The tripartite relationship is somewhat unique in the law, since defense counsel has, in effect, "two masters." He or she (1) has an attorney client relationship with the insured (and in some jurisdictions, with the insurer as well), and (2) is paid by the insurer, which under the CGL policy has both the right to control the defense of the case and the unfettered right to select defense counsel. In the ordinary case where coverage is not in doubt, this arrangement makes perfect sense (it is, after all the *insurer* whose assets are at risk), and problems involving conflicting interests are rare.

In a case where the availability of coverage is in question, however, the insured's interest in the manner in which the case is defended is obvious. Even so, the issuance by the insurer of a reservation of rights does not *automatically* cause the insurer to lose its right to select defense counsel, even though an adverse judgment may not be covered. To take a simple example, assume an insurer undertakes to defend its insured, a carpenter who was hired by a homeowner to construct a wooden deck. Despite the contract calling for clear redwood, the contractor installs knotty redwood with an inferior appearance. The contractor also improperly flashes the transition between the deck and the exterior wall of the residence, resulting in water intrusion into the wall cavity. In his suit, the homeowner not only wants the water damage fixed; he wants the entire deck torn out and re-built with clear redwood.

CONSTRUCTION DEFECT CLAIMS/LITIGATION
A Two Case Study

The insurer will ordinarily recognize coverage for the water damage, and therefore must furnish a full and complete defense to the claim. The insurer ordinarily will, however, reserve the right to deny coverage for the cost to replace the deck since that aspect of the case is not a claim for damages because of "property damage."

Even if the insurer reserves the right to disclaim coverage on that ground, however, it is still free to select defense counsel. That is because defense counsel is not placed in a conflicted position by the reservation of rights. Defense counsel wishes to do the best job he or she can do for his or her client on each aspect (covered and uncovered), of the claim. The insured has no reason to be upset if defense counsel does a great job and defeats the water damage claim (to the benefit of the insurer), and insurer has no reason to be upset if defense counsel does a great job and defeats the claim to replace the entire deck. It's a "win-win." Stated differently, since no step taken by defense counsel in the aggressive representation of the *insured* might tend to harm the *insurer*, and vice-versa, there is no conflict of interest inherent in defense counsel's defending the case, even though a reservation of rights is in place.

In other situations, however, a reservation of rights *can* place defense counsel in a conflicted position. The law in virtually every state is to the effect that a lawyer with a conflict of interest cannot adequately defend his or her client. That leads, in the insurance context, to the conclusion that the insurer which provides a "conflicted" lawyer to defend its insured, is not properly discharging its duty to defend. That is a very serious issue; an insurer which fails to defend its insured (and a conflicted defense is essentially no defense), faces very severe, and in most jurisdictions extra-contractual, liability.

To avoid any such result, the insurer needs to carefully examine the consequences of reserving a given right in the context of the case. If, for example, a plaintiff "over-pleads" its construction defect case and alleges the contractor *deliberately* built a home with multiple defects and did so "willfully and maliciously," (even though all objective evidence available to the insurer indicates the insured did no such thing), then the insurer has an important decision to make. If the insurer (1) fully reserves its rights at the outset, reserving the right to disclaim coverage to the extent damage was not accidental within the "occurrence" definition, and also was "expected or intended" from its insured's standpoint, then many and probably most states would view defense counsel to be placed in a conflicted position. That is so since defense counsel, acting with the improper motive to aid the insurer from whom he or she regularly receives business, might take steps in the defense of the case to "steer" it into a finding of intentionally-caused harm. That would (1) benefit the insurer on coverage, and (2) harm defense counsel's client and leave it without indemnity for the judgment.

It goes without saying that such behavior would subject defense counsel to professional discipline, and possible disbarment. There is a substantial body of thought in this country that the insured's obvious

CONSTRUCTION DEFECT CLAIMS/LITIGATION
A Two Case Study

malpractice remedy against any defense lawyer engaging in such egregious behavior is sufficient, and insurers should not be required to permit the *insured* to select defense counsel in such cases on the notion that "all defense counsel are crooks." Regardless, the so-called "independent counsel" doctrine is alive and well in many jurisdictions, and under that doctrine, the insurer must allow the insured the right to pick defense counsel (typically upon a showing of sufficient experience on counsel's part), and the insurer must pay for that lawyer's services.

It is fair to say that insurers as a whole find working with "independent" counsel in most cases to be less that optimal, with the most common complaint having to do with the issue insurers are most concerned with – the high costs of defense. Accordingly, insurers usually seek to avoid the requirement to offer independent counsel to their insureds where possible.

The simplest way to accomplish that goal is to refrain from reserving rights on grounds which trigger the independent counsel entitlement in the first place. In the example mentioned previously where the plaintiff's counsel over-pled the case as one of deliberately-caused damages, the insurer may wish to refrain from reserving the right to disclaim coverage for intentionally-caused harm when agreeing to defend. Doing so will preserve the insurer's right to select counsel, (but at the cost of losing its opportunity to disclaim coverage for a judgment later if, in fact, the contractor was "guilty as charged").

Another approach the insurer can take is simply to deny coverage outright for certain damages or relief (rather than reserving the right to disclaim coverage), since if the insurer's assertion of its coverage position leaves defense counsel without the power to affect the outcome of the coverage question, defense counsel cannot be said to occupy a conflicted position. As an example, lawyers for plaintiffs in construction defect cases often sue contractors under both negligence and breach of contract causes of action. Some will go farther, and add a fraud cause of action. Fraud as a legal theory being what it is, an insurer which carelessly reserves rights to disclaim coverage in such a case entirely, because of the fraud claim, may be required to offer independent counsel unnecessarily. If, instead, the insurer <u>accepts</u> coverage at the outset for compensatory damages as may be awarded at trial, but <u>disclaims</u> coverage only to the extent of any additional damages as may be awarded *solely* under the fraud theory, defense counsel is powerless to affect the outcome of the coverage question, and the insurer is at least arguably able to retain control of the defense through counsel of its choosing.

For obvious reasons, whether to purposely omit grounds for reserving rights in order to avoid an independent counsel requirement, or alternative to take a more nuanced approach of accepting coverage for some damages and denying coverage for others, is a decision the insurer should make only after careful consideration.

***

CONSTRUCTION DEFECT CLAIMS/LITIGATION
A Two Case Study

The forgoing was intended as a general discussion of the reservation of rights concept as it pertains to the defense, by CGL insurers, of their insureds in construction defect litigation. It goes without saying that there is not only substantial variation between the laws of the fifty states in this area, but no two cases are alike even in the same jurisdiction. Whether one represents the interests of the insurer, or the interests of one who wants the insurer's money, this area of practice presents great challenges.

James M. McFaul
MINEHAN, McFAUL & FITCH, LLP
B.A. U.C.L.A. 1973
J.D. LOYOLA LAW SCHOOL 1978

Practice limited to the analysis and litigation of insurance coverage matters.

Appendix B

(Reservation of Rights - Sample Letter from actual case)

SENT BY CERTIFIED MAIL AND REGULAR MAIL

January 25, 2005

ACME General Contractors, Inc.

RE: *Redacted* **V.** *Redacted*

RESERVATION OF RIGHTS LETTER

THE CONTENTS OF THIS LETTER ARE INTENDED TO ADVISE YOU OF POTENTIAL PROBLEMS WITH COVERAGE AVAILABLE UNDER YOUR POLICY. PLEASE READ THIS LETTER AND YOUR INSURANCE POLICY CAREFULLY.

Dear Mr. *Redacted*:

This will re-introduce *Redacted*, an independent adjusting company retained by *Redacted*, the underwriting managers for *Redacted*, to investigate the above captioned claim. Please direct all inquiries regarding this letter to the undersigned.

On October 2, 2004 a **RESERVATION OF RIGHTS LETTER** was faxed to you and also was sent to you by certified mail and regular mail. The October 2, 2004 letter in its entirety is incorporated into this

RESERVATION OF RIGHTS LETTER as if it was part of this letter. In the event you did not receive a copy of that letter please let us know as soon as possible.

Our investigation to date indicates that you and the plaintiff *Redacted* are or were friends and together formed a construction company by the name of *Redacted* Building. You were and to your knowledge still are an officer and director in *Redacted* Building. The Defendant/Cross Complainant *Redacted* wanted to remodel his personal residence and then sell it. He contacted *Redacted* and yourself as principals in *Redacted* Building to use that firm to pull the necessary building permits to complete the remodeling of his personal residence. The Defendant/Cross Complainant also wanted to use construction crews from *Redacted* Building to do the construction work and he would be the general contractor during the remodeling work.

As *Redacted* Building had just been formed they had not obtained their contractor license from the State of California. For that reason the Defendant/Cross Complainant approached *Redacted* sometime in 2002 to use their construction license to pull the building permits. The Defendant/Cross Complainant approached you personally to assist him as a building consultant during the remodeling of his personal residence. There was no written contract between *Redacted* or yourself and the Defendant/Cross Complainants for the construction work completed on their personal residence. You would visit the construction site approximately two times a month and would provide the construction guidance you believed was necessary, if any. You were never paid for your consulting work during the remodeling. All of the construction crews utilized by the Defendant/Cross Complainants were obtained through the plaintiff *Redacted* and *Redacted* Building. Other than yourself no personnel from *Redacted* were utilized during the remodeling work completed by the Defendant/Cross Complainants.

On June 25, 2002 with the permission of the Defendant/Cross Complainants *Redacted* made an application for building permits for *Redacted*, which is the subject of the litigation. Included with the documents we obtained during our investigation is a record of the remodeling for this address from the City Department of Building Inspection. This document contains the following sign off dates for various construction activities; 7-17-02, 9-16-02, 11-14-02, 12-15-02, at that address. We also obtained a signed Certificate of Final Completion & Occupancy for *Redacted* dated January 15, 2003.

We are in receipt of a complaint titled *Redacted* v. *Redacted* filed on 2-19-04 in the Superior Court of California, County of *Redacted* with a case number of *Redacted* The complaint alleges breach of contract and fraud and is seeking $XYZ,000 in damages. In addition the plaintiff is seeking interest and attorney fees. The plaintiff alleges that he loaned $XYZ,000 to the defendant on August 11, 2003 for remodeling work on the defendant's home located at *Redacted* The defendant allegedly agreed to pay monthly payments of $XYZ.00 until paid in full. The complaint goes on to allege that the defendant failed to make the monthly payments of $XYZ.00 as agreed. It further alleges the plaintiff made no effort to pay back the money lent by the plaintiff. The complaint also alleges that the defendant defrauded the plaintiff on August 11, 2003 as he never had any intention of paying back the $XYZ,000 loan. Based on our investigation to date there is no indication that *Redacted* & Associates, Inc. or *Redacted* had any involvement in this financial transaction. If further investigation indicates that & Associates, Inc. and or *Redacted*, individually were involved in this financial transaction *Redacted* Insurance Company reserves the right to amend this reservation of rights letter.

We are also in receipt of a First Amended Cross Complaint which is referenced above filed in the Superior Court of California, County of *Redacted* with a case number of *Redacted*. Included with the cross complaint was a proof of service of a summons filed in the *Redacted* County Superior Court on February 10, 2008 referencing case number *Redacted*. The proof of service indicates that substituted service was effected on February 1, 2005. The party to be served with the cross complaint was *Redacted* and Associates, Inc. aka *Redacted* and Associates General Contractor, Inc. In a telephone conversation you related to the undersigned that you have also been sued personally in the Cross Complaint by the Defendant/Cross Complainants. The First Amended Cross Complaint contains the following causes of action: (1) Restitution of Payments; (2) Breach of Contract; (3) Negligence; (4) Restitution; (5) Fraud; (6) Declaratory Relief; (7) Unfair Business Practices; (8) License Revocation.

Redacted Insurance Company issued Policy No. *Redacted* effective June 7, 2002 to June 7, 2003 to *Redacted* & Associates, Inc. The policy includes a $1,000,000 each Occurrence Limit for General Liability and a $2,000,000 Products-Completed Operations Aggregate Limit of Liability. This policy also contains a $5,000 Per Claim deductible for both bodily injury and property damage. Benefits are now being claimed under this policy. *Redacted* & Associates, Inc. and *Redacted*, individually have tendered the First Amended Cross Complaint to *Redacted* Insurance Company requesting a defense and indemnity for the Defendant/Cross Complainant's allegations.

In summary form, *Redacted* Insurance Company will, currently, continue to defend you and your company in this matter, but there are very significant questions regarding whether *Redacted* Insurance Company has any obligation to indemnify you and/or your company to independent counsel under Civil Code section 2860. California law allows *Redacted* & Associates, Inc. and *Redacted*, individually to select independent defense counsel of their own choice to represent them unless they expressly waive, in writing, their right to independent counsel. If you select independent counsel to represent either *Redacted* & Associates and or yourself *Redacted* Insurance Company, pursuant to Civil Code Section 2860, has the right to require that counsel selected by you comply with the following minimum requirements:

1. At least five years of civil litigation practice which includes substantial defense experience in the subject at issue in the litigation.

2. Errors and Omissions coverage.

Pursuant to Civil Code Section 2860 *Redacted* Insurance Company's obligation to pay fees to the independent counsel selected by you is limited to the rates which are actually paid by them to attorneys they retain in the ordinary course of business in the defense of similar actions in the community where the claim arose.

We respectfully call to your attention *Redacted* Policy No. *Redacted* which includes form number CG 0001 12 07, which states in pertinent part:

COMMERCIAL GENERAL LIABILITY COVERAGE FORM

SECTION I – COVERAGES
COVERAGE A BODILY INJURY AND PROPERTY DAMAGE LIABILITY

1. **Insuring Agreement**

   a. We will pay those sums that the insured becomes legally obligated to pay as damages because of "bodily injury" or "property damage" to which this insurance applies. We will have the right and duty to defend the insured against any "suit" seeking those damages. However, we will have no duty to defend the insured against any "suit" seeking damages for "bodily injury" or "property damage" to which this insurance does not apply. We may, at our discretion, investigate any "occurrence" and settle any claim or "suit" that may result. But:

(1) The amount we will pay for damages is limited as described in Section **III** – Limits Of Insurance; and

(2) Our right and duty to defend ends when we have used up the applicable limit of insurance in the payment of judgments or settlements under Coverages **A** or **B** or medical expenses under Coverage **C.**

No other obligation or liability to pay sums or perform acts or services is covered unless explicitly provided for under Supplementary Payments – Coverages **A** and **B.**

b. This insurance applies to "bodily injury" and "property damage" only if:

(1) The "bodily injury" or "property damage" is caused by an "occurrence" that takes place in the "coverage territory";

(2) The "bodily injury" or "property damage" occurs during the policy period;

and

(3) Prior to the policy period, no insured listed under Paragraph

1. of Section **II** – Who Is An Insured and no "employee" authorized by you to give or receive notice of an "occurrence" or claim, knew that the "bodily injury" or "property damage" had occurred, in whole or in part. If such a listed insured or authorized "employee" knew, prior to the policy period, that the "bodily injury" or "property damage" occurred, then any continuation, change or resumption of such "bodily injury" or "property damage" during or after the policy period will be deemed to have been known prior to the policy period.

c.   "Bodily injury" or "property damage" which occurs during the policy period and was not, prior to the policy period, known to have occurred by any insured listed under Paragraph **1.** of Section **II** – Who Is An Insured or any "employee" authorized by you to give or receive notice of an "occurrence" or claim, includes any continuation, change or resumption of that "bodily injury" or "property damage" after the end of the policy period.

d.   "Bodily injury" or "property damage" will be deemed to have been known to have occurred at the earliest time when any insured listed under Paragraph **1.** of Section **II** –

Who Is An Insured or any "employee" authorized by you to give or receive notice of an "occurrence" or claim:

(1) Reports all, or any part, of the "bodily injury" or "property damage" to us or any other insurer;

(2) Receives a written or verbal demand or claim for damages because of the "bodily injury" or "property damage"; or

(3) Becomes aware by any other means that "bodily injury" or "property damage" has occurred or has begun to occur."

There are also exclusions that may be applicable to the claim. These exclusions are found in the policy as follows:

b. Contractual Liability

"Bodily injury" or "property damage" for which the insured is obligated to pay damages by reason of the assumption of liability in a contract or agreement. This exclusion does not apply to liability for damages:

(1) That the insured would have in the absence of the contract or agreement; or

(2) Assumed in a contract or agreement that is an "insured

contract", provided the "bodily injury" or "property damage" occurs subsequent to the execution of the contract or agreement. Solely for the purposes of liability assumed in an "insured contract", reasonable attorney fees and necessary litigation expenses incurred by or for a party other than an insured are deemed to be damages because of "bodily injury" or "property damage", provided:

(a)   Liability to such party for, or for the cost of, that party's defense has also been assumed in the same "insured contract"; and

(b)   Such attorney fees and litigation expenses are for defense of that party against a civil or alternative dispute resolution proceeding in which damages to which this insurance applies are alleged.

j.   **Damage To Property** "Property damage" to:

(1)   Property you own, rent, or occupy, including any costs or expenses incurred by you, or any other person, organization or

entity, for repair, replacement, enhancement, restoration or maintenance of such property for any reason, including prevention of injury to a person or damage to another's property;

(2) Premises you sell, give away or abandon, if the "property damage" arises out of any part of those premises;

(3) Property loaned to you;

(4) Personal property in the care, custody or control of the insured;

(5) That particular part of real property on which you or any contractors or subcontractors working directly or indirectly on your behalf are performing operations, if the "property damage" arises out of those operations; or

(6) That particular part of any property that must be restored, repaired or replaced because "your work" was incorrectly performed on it.

Paragraphs (1), (3) and (4) of this exclusion do not apply to "property damage" (other than damage by fire) to premises, including the contents of such premises, rented to you for a period of 7 or fewer consecutive days. A separate limit of insurance applies to Damage To Premises Rented To You as described in Section III – Limits Of Insurance

Paragraph (2) of this exclusion does not apply if

the premises are "your work" and were never occupied, rented or held for rental by you.

Paragraphs (3), (4), (5) and (6) of this exclusion do not apply to liability assumed under a sidetrack agreement.

Paragraph (6) of this exclusion does not apply to "property damage" included in the "products-completed operations hazard".

k.   **Damage To Your Product**

"Property damage" to "your product" arising out of it or any part of it.

l.   **Damage To Your Work**

"Property damage" to "your work" arising out of it or any part of it and included in the "products-completed operations hazard".

This exclusion does not apply if the damaged work or the work out of which the damage arises was performed on your behalf by a subcontractor.

m.   **Damage To Impaired Property Or Property Not Physically Injured**

"Property damage" to "impaired property" or property that has not been physically injured, arising out of:

(1)   A defect, deficiency, inadequacy or dangerous condition in "your product" or "your work"; or

(2)   A delay or failure by you or anyone acting on your behalf to perform a contract or agreement in accordance with its terms.

This exclusion does not apply to the loss of use of other property arising out of sudden and accidental physical injury to "your product" or "your work" after it has been put to its intended use.

n. **Recall Of Products, Work Or Impaired Property**

Damages claimed for any loss, cost or expense incurred by you or others for the loss of use, withdrawal, recall, inspection, repair, replacement, adjustment, removal or disposal of:

(1)   "Your product";
(2)   "Your work"; or
(3)   "Impaired property";

if such product, work, or property is withdrawn or recalled from the market or from use by any person or organization because of a known or suspected defect, deficiency, inadequacy or dangerous condition in it.

The terms in quotations marks are identified in the policy as follows:

SECTION V - DEFINITIONS

7. "Bodily injury" means bodily injury, sickness or disease sustained by a person, including death resulting from any of these at any time.

8. "Impaired property" means tangible property, other than "your product" or "your work", that cannot be used or is less useful because:

a. It incorporates "your product" or "your work" that is known or thought to be defective, deficient, inadequate or dangerous; or

b. You have failed to fulfill the terms of a contract or agreement; if such property can be restored to use by the repair, replacement, adjustment or removal of "your product" or "your work" or your fulfilling the terms of the contract or agreement.

9. **"Insured contract" means:**

a. A contract for a lease of premises. However, that portion of the contract for a lease of premises that indemnifies any person or organization for damage by fire to premises while rented to you or temporarily occupied by you with permission of the owner is not an "insured contract";

b. sidetrack agreement;

c. Any easement or license agreement, except in connection with construction or demolition operations on or within 50 feet of a railroad;

d. An obligation, as required by ordinance, to indemnify a municipality, except in connection with work for a municipality;

e. An elevator maintenance agreement;

f. That part of any other contract or agreement pertaining to your business (including an indemnification of a municipality in connection with work performed for a municipality) under which you assume the tort liability of another party to pay for "bodily injury" or "property damage" to a third person or organization. Tort liability means a liability that would be imposed by law in the absence of any contract or agreement.

Paragraph f. does not include that part of any contract or agreement:

(1) That indemnifies a railroad for "bodily injury" or "property damage" arising out of construction or demolition operations, within 50 feet of any railroad property and affecting any railroad bridge or trestle, tracks, road-beds, tunnel, underpass or crossing;

(2) That indemnifies an architect, engineer or surveyor for injury or damage arising out of:

    (a) Preparing, approving, or failing to prepare or approve, maps, shop drawings, opinions, reports, surveys, field orders, change orders or drawings and specifications; or

    (b) Giving directions or instructions, or failing to give them, if that is the primary cause of the injury or damage; or

(3) Under which the insured, if an

architect, engineer or surveyor, assumes liability for an injury or damage arising out of the insured's rendering or failure to render professional services, including those listed in (2) above and supervisory, inspection, architectural or engineering activities.

10. "Occurrence" means an accident, including continuous or repeated exposure to substantially the same general harmful conditions.

11. "Products-completed operations hazard":

   a. Includes all "bodily injury" and "property damage" occurring away from premises you own or rent and arising out of "your product" or "your work" except:

   (1) Products that are still in your physical possession; or

   (2) Work that has not yet been completed or abandoned. However, "your work" will be deemed completed at the earliest of the following times:

   (a) When all of the work called for in your contract has been completed.

   (b) When all of the work to be done at the job site has been completed if your contract calls for work at more than one job site.

   (c) When that part of the work done at a job site has been put to its intended use by any person or organization other than another contractor or subcontractor working on the same project. Work that may need service, maintenance, correction, repair or replacement, but which is otherwise complete, will be treated as completed.

b. Does not include "bodily injury" or "property damage" arising out of:

(1) The transportation of property, unless the injury or damage arises out of a condition in or on a vehicle not owned or operated by you, and that condition was created by the "loading or unloading" of that vehicle by any insured;

(2) The existence of tools, uninstalled equipment or abandoned or unused materials; or

(3) Products or operations for which the classification, listed in the Declarations or in a policy schedule, states that products completed operations are subject to the General Aggregate Limit.

12. "Property damage" means:

a. Physical injury to tangible property, including all resulting loss of use of that property. All such loss of use shall be deemed to occur at the time of the physical injury that caused it; or

b. Loss of use of tangible property that is not physically injured. All such loss of use shall be deemed to occur at the time of the "occurrence" that caused it.

For the purposes of this insurance, electronic data is not tangible property. As used in this definition, electronic data means information, facts or programs stored as or on, created or used on, or transmitted to or from computer software, including systems and applications software, hard or floppy disks, CD-ROMS, tapes, drives, cells, data processing devices or any other media which are used with electronically controlled equipment.

13. "Suit" means a civil proceeding in which damages because of "bodily injury", "property damage" or "personal and advertising injury" to which this insurance applies are alleged "Suit" includes:

a. An arbitration proceeding in which such damages are claimed and to which the insured must submit or does submit with our consent; or

b. Any other alternative dispute resolution proceeding in which such damages are claimed and to which the insured submits with our consent.

14. "Your product":

a. Means:

(1) Any goods or products, other than real property, manufactured, sold, handled, distributed or disposed of by:

(a) You;

(b) Others trading under your name; or

(c) A person or organization whose business or assets you have acquired; and

(2) Containers (other than vehicles), materials, parts or equipment furnished in connection with such goods or products.

b. Includes:

    (1) Warranties or representations made at any time with respect to the fitness, quality, durability, performance or use of "your product"; and

    (2) The providing of or failure to provide warnings or instructions.

c. Does not include vending machines or other property rented to or located for the use of others but not sold.

15. "Your work":

    a. Means:

        (1) Work or operations performed by you or on your behalf; and

        (2) Materials, parts or equipment furnished in connection with such work or operations.

    b. Includes:

        (1) Warranties or representations made at any time with respect to the fitness, quality, durability, performance or use of "your work", and

(2)   The providing of or failure to provide warnings or instructions.

The policy provides coverage only if there is "property damage" and/or "bodily injury" that occurs during the policy period. There is no coverage under the policy for any damages claimed as a result of the insured's failing to fulfill the terms of a contract or agreement, if such damages do not constitute "bodily injury or "property damage" arising from an "occurrence", as defined in the policy.

In addition to the above-mentioned limitations contained in Form CG 0001 12 07, the following endorsements, contained within the subject policy issued to Curran & Associates, Inc. by Gemini Insurance Company, might fundamentally exclude coverage for this matter under the subject policy:

Policy Number: *Redacted*
Insured Name: *Redacted* & ASSOCIATES, INC. Effective Date: 06/07/2002

THIS ENDORSEMENT CHANGES THE POLICY. PLEASE READ IT CAREFULLY.

PUNITIVE DAMAGE EXCLUSION

This endorsement modifies insurance provided under the following:

COMMERCIAL GENERAL LIABILITY COVERAGE PART OWNERS AND CONTRACTORS PROTECTIVE LIABILITY COVERAGE PART PRODUCTS/COMPLETED OPERATIONS LIABILITY COVERAGE PART

It is agreed that the insurance afforded by this policy does not apply to punitive or exemplary damages awarded against the Insured.

Policy Number: *Redacted*
Form Number: *Redacted*
Insured Name: *Redacted* & ASSOCIATES

**THIS ENDORSEMENT CHANGES THE POLICY.
PLEASE READ IT CAREFULLY.**

PROFESSIONAL LIABILITY EXCLUSION

This endorsement modifies insurance provided under the following:

COMMERCIAL GENERAL LIABILITY COVERAGE PART
PRODUCTS/COMPLETED OPERATIONS LIABILITY COVERAGE PART

It is agreed that such insurance as is afforded by this policy shall not apply to any error or omission, malpractice or mistake of a professional nature committed or alleged to have been committed by or on behalf of any insured in the conduct of any of an insured's business activities.

Policy Number: *Redacted*
Form Number: *Redacted*
Insured Name: *Redacted* & ASSOCIATES
Effective Date: 06/07/2008

**THIS ENDORSEMENT CHANGES THE POLICY.
PLEASE READ IT CAREFULLY.**

PRIOR ACTS EXCLUSION

This endorsement modifies insurance provided under the following:

> COMMERCIAL GENERAL LIABILITY COVERAGE PART PRODUCTS/COMPLETED OPERATIONS LIABILITY COVERAGE PART

This insurance does not apply to any "bodily injury", "property damage", "personal or advertising injury" liability arising out of projects completed and/or "your work" or "your product" sold prior to 6/7/2008.

We have no duty to defend any insured against any loss claim, "suit", or other proceeding alleging damages arising out of or related to "bodily injury" "property damage", "personal injury" or "advertising injury" which arises out of projects completed and/or "your work" or "your product" sold prior to 6/7/2008 to which this exclusion applies.

Policy Number: *Redacted*
Form Number: *Redacted*
Insured Name: *Redacted* & ASSOCIATES, INC.
Effective Date:

THIS ENDORSEMENT CHANGES THE POLICY. PLEASE READ IT CAREULLY.

EXCLUSION – CONTINUOUS OR PROGRESSIVE DAMAGE CLAIMS

This endorsement modifies insurance provided under the following:

COMMERCIAL GENERAL LIABILITY COVERAGE PART PRODUCTS/COMPLETED OPERATIONS LIABILITY COVERAGE PART

In the event of any claim against the insured for bodily injury, property damage, personal injury or advertising injury which is or is alleged to be continuing in nature, this policy shall not apply to any such claim if the damage or any portion of it began or is alleged to have begun prior to the date that this policy becomes effective. This exclusion shall apply whether or not the cause of the alleged damages was known prior to the effective date of the policy.

We have no duty to defend any insured against any loss, claim, "suit", or other proceeding alleging damages arising out of or related to "bodily injury" "property damage", "personal injury" or "advertising injury" to which this exclusion applies.

Policy Number: *Redacted*
Form Number: *Redacted*
Insured Name: *Redacted* & ASSOCIATES, INC.
Effective Date: 06/07/2002

THIS ENDORSEMENT CHANGES THE POLICY. PLEASE READ IT CAREFULLY.

FUNGUS OR SPORE EXCLUSION

This endorsement modifies insurance provided under the following:

CONSTRUCTION DEFECT CLAIMS/LITIGATION
A Two Case Study

COMMERCIAL GENERAL LIABILITY COVERAGE PART
OWNERS AND CONTRACTORS PROTECTIVE LIABILITY
COVERAGE PART
PRODUCTS/COMPLETED OPERATIONS LIABILITY
COVERAGE PART

> This insurance does not apply to:
> (1)"Bodily injury", "property damage", or personal
> and advertising injury" caused directly or indirectly, in whole or in part, by:
> a.   Any "fungus" or "spore, including fungi or spores; or
> b.   Any substance, vapor or gas produced by or arising out of any fungus , fungi "spore", or "spores"; or
> c.   Any material, product, building component, building or structure that contains, harbors, nurtures or acts as a medium for any "fungus", "fungi", "spore" or "spores; or
>
> Actual, alleged or threatened discharge, dispersal, seepage, migration, release or escape of fungus or spore, including "fungi" or "spores".
> Such damage or injury is excluded regardless of any other cause, event, material, product and/or building component that contributed concurrently or in any sequence to that injury or damage.

(2)   Any loss, cost or expense arising out of any:

a.   Request, demand, order or statutory or regulatory requirement that any insured or others test for, monitor, clean up, remove, contain, treat, detoxify or neutralize, or in any way respond to, or assess "fungus "fungi", "Spares", or "spores" or the effects of same (including, but not limited to, any form or type of mold, mildew, mushroom, toadstool, smut, or rust)

b.   Claim or "suit by or on behalf of a governmental authority for damages because of testing for, monitoring, cleaning up, removing, containing, treating, detoxifying or neutralizing, or in any way responding to, or assessing fungus", 'fungi "spore", or "spores" or the effects of same (including, but not limited to, any form or type of mold, mildew, mushroom, toadstool, smut, rust).

(3)   With respect to this endorsement, Exclusion **2.b – Contractual Liability** is replaced by the following:

b.   "Bodily injury" or "property damage" for which the insured is obligated to pay damages by reason of the assumption of liability in a contract or agreement.

We shall have no duty to investigate, defend or Indemnify any insured against any loss, claim, "suit", or other proceeding alleging injury or damages of any kind, to include, but not limited to, "bodily injury", "property damage", or "personal and advertising injury" to which this endorsement applies.

Additional Definitions:

For the purpose of this endorsement, the following definitions are added:

"Fungus" and/or "fungi" includes, but is not limited to, any form or type of mold, mildew, mushroom, toadstool, smut, or rust.

"Spore" and/or "spores" means any reproductive body produced by or arising out of any "fungus" or "fungi".

Policy Number: *Redacted*
Form Number: *Redacted*
Insured Name: *Redacted* & ASSOCIATES, INC.
Effective Date: 06/07/2002

THIS ENDORSEMENT CHANGES THE POLICY. PLEASE READ IT CAREFULLY.

ABSOLUTE EARTH MOVEMENT EXCLUSION

This endorsement modifies insurance provided under

the following:

COMMERCIAL GENERAL LIABILITY COVERAGE PART
PRODUCTS/COMPLETED OPERATIONS LIABILITY
COVERAGE PART

This insurance does not apply to any "bodily injury",
"property damage", "personal injury" or "advertising
injury" arising out of subsidence, settling, bulging,
shrinkage, earthquake, expansion, contraction, shaking,
sinking, slipping, falling away, caving in,
shifting, eroding, mud flow, rising, tilting, or any other
movement of land, soil, bedrock or earth from any
cause whatsoever.

We have no duty to defend any insured against any loss,
claim or "suit" or other proceeding alleging damages
arising out of or related to "bodily injury", "property
damage", "personal injury" or "advertising injury" to
which this exclusion applies.

Insured Name: *Redacted* **& ASSOCIATES, INC.**
Effective Date: 06/07/2002

**THIS ENDORSEMENT CHANGES THE POLICY.
PLEASE READ IT CAREFULLY.**

EIFS EXCLUSION

This endorsement modifies insurance provided under
the following:

COMMERCIAL GENERAL LIABILITY COVERAGE PART

CONSTRUCTION DEFECT CLAIMS/LITIGATION
A Two Case Study

PRODUCTS/COMPLETED OPERATIONS LIABILITY COVERAGE PART

It is agreed that this insurance does not apply to and we shall have no duty or obligation to defend or indemnify any insured as to any "bodily injury," "property damage" or "personal injury" arising out of or alleged to arise out of:

1. The design, manufacture, construction, fabrication, preparation, installation, application, maintenance or repair including remodeling, service, correction, or replacement of, an "exterior insulation and finish system" (commonly referred to as synthetic stucco) or any part thereof, or any substantially similar system or any part thereof, including the application or use of conditioners, primers, accessories, flashings, coatings, caulkings or sealants in connection with such a system.

2. Any work or operations with respect to any exterior component, fixture or feature of any structure if an "exterior insulation and finish system" is used on any part of that structure.

For the purpose of this endorsement an "exterior insulation and finish system" means an exterior cladding or finish system used on any part of any structure and consisting of:
   a) a rigid or semi-rigid insulation board made of expended polystyrene or other materials; and
   b) an adhesive and/or mechanical fasteners used to attach the insulation board to the substrate; and
   c) a reinforced base coat; and

d) a finish coat providing surface texture and color.

The First Amended Cross Complaint contains the following causes of action: (1) Restitution of Payments; (2) Breach of Contract; (3) Negligence; (4) Restitution; (5) Fraud; (6) Declaratory Relief; (7) Unfair Business Practices; and (8) License Revocation.

The first cause of action in the First Amended Cross Complaint is for "Restitution of Payments" against *Redacted* and Roes. The Cross-Complainants are alleging that the contract is unenforceable by plaintiff because it fails to comply with the requirements of California Business & Professions Code Section 7159 and in violation of the public policy expressed therein. It further alleges that none of the Cross Defendants or their subcontractors were duly licensed during their performance of work on the Cross- Complainants property as required by Business & Professions Code 7000. The Cross- Complainants are demanding the return of all consideration paid to Cross Defendants and *Redacted* and Roes 1 to 100. The allegations contained in this cause of action and the damages and or relief being sought by the Defendant/Cross-Complainants do not constitute "bodily injury" or "property damage" arising from an "occurrence" as defined in policy number *Redacted*. Accordingly, if proven, *Redacted* Insurance Company will not satisfy an award based on this cause of action.

The second cause of action in the First Amended Cross Complaint is for "Breach of Contract" against *Redacted*, and Roes. The Cross-Complainants are alleging that Cross Defendant *Redacted* and Roes 1 to 100 breached the contract by, among other things:

1. Failing to complete the construction of the project despite an agreed upon completion date;
2. Failing to build the project in accordance with the plans and specifications for the construction of the project as called for under the CONTRACT;
3. Performing much of the construction work called for under the contract in such a substantially defective manner that the PROPERTY was not and is still not fully habitable or usable;
4. By abandoning the project altogether through Cross-Defendant *Redacted* and Roe's failure to complete the work and to correct defects in the construction after such defects were discovered;
5. Using unlicensed subcontractors, and;
6. Failing to reimburse to Cross-Complainant for amounts expended by Cross-Complainants for the work and to complete portions of the work under the CONTRACT; Cross-Complainants are alleging they have been damaged due to the breach of contract and are seeking at least $200,000 according to proof. The policy issued to *Redacted* & Associates, Inc. provides coverage only if there is "property damage" and/or "bodily injury" that occurs during the policy period. There is no coverage under the policy for any damages claimed as a result of the insured's failing to fulfill the terms of a contract or agreement, if such damages do not constitute "bodily injury" or "property damage" arising from an "occurrence", as defined in the policy. *Redacted* Insurance Company will not indemnify an award based on this cause of

action, absent evidence of an occurrence resulting in either property damage or bodily injury.

The third cause of action in the First Amended Cross Complaint is for "Negligence" against *Redacted* and Roes. The Cross-Complainants are alleging that the Cross-Defendants performed work on the PROJECT which was materially defective in workmanship. The Cross-Complainants are seeking at least $200,000 in damages for repairs and for an alleged reduction in the value of the PROPERTY. The policy issued to *Redacted* & Associates, Inc. provides coverage only if there is "property damage" and/or "bodily injury" that occurs during the policy period. There is no coverage under the policy for any damages claimed as a result of the insured's failing to fulfill the terms of a contract or agreement, if such damages do not constitute "bodily injury" or "property damage" arising from an "occurrence", as defined in the policy.

The fourth cause of action in the First Amended Cross Complaint is for "Restitution" against the Cross-Defendants. The Cross-Complainants are alleging that the Cross-Defendants failed to obtain and maintain policies of workers compensation insurance for their employees and independent contractors in violation of California Business & Professions Code Section 7125 et seq. The Cross-Complainants further allege that as a result of this violation that the Cross-Defendants contractors license is automatically suspended by operation of law under Business & Professions Code section 7125.2(a)(2). The Cross-Complainants are seeking restitution of all amounts paid to Cross-

Defendants in payment for any construction work performed by them on the PROJECT under Business & Professions Code 7031(b). The allegations contained in this cause of action and the damages and or relief being sought by the Defendant/Cross-Complainants do not constitute "bodily injury" or "property damage" arising from an "occurrence" as defined in policy number *Redacted* Insurance Company will not indemnify you or your company for this cause of action and the damages and or relief being sought. *Redacted* Insurance Company does not have a duty to either defend or indemnify *Redacted* & Associates, Inc. or *Redacted* individually for this cause of action.

The fifth cause of action in the First Amended Cross Complaint is for "Fraud" against *Redacted* and Roes. The Cross-Complainants are alleging false and fraudulent representations were made by the Plaintiff which induced Cross-Complainants to enter into an oral CONTRACT with Cross-Defendants or allowed Cross-Defendants to perform work on their PROPERTY. The allegations contained in this cause of action and the damages and or relief being sought by the Defendant/Cross-Complainants do not constitute "bodily injury" or "property damage" arising from an "occurrence" as defined in policy number *Redacted*. Insurance Company will not indemnify you or your company for this cause of action and the damages and or relief being sought.

The sixth cause of action in the First Amended Cross Complaint is for "Declaratory Relief" against *Redacted* and Roes. The Cross-Complainants are alleging there is an actual controversy in law and equity between the parties as to the validity of the "loan agreements" signed by the Cross-Complainants to finance the construction work performed by the Cross-Defendants. The Cross-Complainants are seeking a declaration of their rights by the court seeking relief under Business & Professions Code Sections 7031, 7159 et seq as to the validity or whether there was adequate consideration in exchange for their promises under such agreements. The allegations contained in this cause of action and the damages and or relief being sought by the Defendant/Cross-Complainants do not involve "bodily injury" or "property damage" arising from an "occurrence" as defined in policy number *Redacted*. *Redacted* Insurance Company will not indemnify an award based on this cause of action against you or your company

The seventh cause of action in the First Amended Cross Complaint is for "Unfair Business Practices against *Redacted* and Roes. The Cross-Complainants are alleging that Cross-Defendants *Redacted* and Roes performed work on Cross-Complainants' PROPERTY with unlicensed subcontractors or independent contractors below the standard of care, failed to complete or repair their defective work, and made false and fraudulent representations in violation of Business & Professions Code Sections 7030, 7107, 7109, 7110, 7113, 7114, 7115, 7116, 7125 et seq, 7125.4, 7159 et seq, 7160, and 17200 et seq. The Cross-Complainants are also alleging that Cross-Defendants work was performed without workers compensation insurance and thus without a valid contractors license or with a suspended contractors license in violation of Business & Professions Code

Sections 7114, 7125, 7125.2(a), 7027, and 7028. The Cross-Complainants further allege that Cross-Defendants work or activities constitute fraudulent and unfair business practices within the meaning of Business & Professions Code Section 17200, et seq. The Cross Complainants are also seeking the issuance of temporary, preliminary, and permanent injunctions and orders of restitution for such unlawful, fraudulent, and unfair business practices alleging violations of Business & Professions Code Sections 17200 and 17203. In addition to seeking injunctions the Cross-Complainants are also seeking restitution of all sums received by Cross-Defendants. The allegations contained in this cause of action and the damages and or relief being sought by the Defendant/Cross-Complainants do not constitute "bodily injury" or "property damage" arising from an "occurrence" as defined in policy number *Redacted*. *Redacted* Insurance Company will not indemnify an award based on this cause of action against you or your company .

The last cause of action is titled the Ninth Cause of Action in the First Amended Cross Complaint and is for "License Revocation" against *Redacted*. and Cross-Defendants. The First Amended Cross Complaint does not contain an Eighth Cause of Action. The Cross-Complainants allege that based on the acts heretofore alleged that the Cross-Defendants and *Redacted* violated Business & Professions Code Sections 7027, 7028, 7030, 7107, 7109, 7110, 7113, 7114, 7115, 7116, 7119, 7125 et seq, 7125.2 (a), 7125.4, 7159 et seq, and 7160 which constitutes a misdemeanor and is cause for disciplinary action by the Contractors State License Board. The Cross-Complainants are relying on

Business & Professions Code Sections 7106 and 7090 in requesting that the court revoke or suspend the Cross-Defendants contractor licenses. The allegations contained in this cause of action and the damages and or relief being sought by the Defendant/Cross-Complainants do not constitute "bodily injury" or "property damage" arising from an "occurrence" as defined in policy number *Redacted*. *Redacted* Insurance Company will not indemnify an award based on this cause of action against you or your company.

The Cross-Complainants are seeking an award for exemplary and punitive damages against the Cross-Defendants according to proof. Exclusionary endorsement *Redacted* which is part of the policy issued to *Redacted* & Associates, Inc. and included earlier in this letter clearly indicates there is no coverage for exemplary and or punitive damages. If the court awards exemplary and or punitive damages to the Defendants/Cross-Complainants; *Redacted* & Associates, Inc. and or *Redacted*, individually would be solely responsible for their payment. You may want to consult your own personal attorney, at your own expense, regarding a potential award of exemplary and or punitive damages to the Cross-Complainants.

The Cross-Complainants are also seeking damages for loss of use of the PROPERTY. The policy issued to *Redacted* & Associates, Inc. provides coverage only if there is "property damage" and/or "bodily injury" that occurs during the policy period. There is no coverage under the policy for any damages claimed as a result of the insured's failing to fulfill the terms of a contract or agreement, if such damages do not constitute "bodily injury" or "property damage" arising from an "occurrence", as defined in the policy.

In addition the Cross-Complainants are seeking attorney fees and costs, expert, technical, and investigatory fees against the Cross-Defendants and *Redacted* pursuant to Code of Civil Procedure Section 1029.8 and Business & Professions Code Section 7160. The Cross-Complainants are also seeking treble damages against the Cross-Defendants per Code of Civil Procedure Section 1029.8. There would be no coverage under the policy issued to *Redacted* & Associates, Inc. for any damages that do not constitute "bodily injury" or "property damage" arising from an "occurrence", as defined in the policy.

Redacted & Associates, Inc.'s interests and *Redacted* Insurance Company's interests might be best served and protected by an ongoing investigation of the facts concerning the questions of coverage and *Redacted* & Associates, Inc.'s potential liability. Therefore, *Redacted* Insurance Company will continue to investigate and provide a defense to *Redacted* & Associates, Inc.'s under your policy *Redacted*, under a full and complete reservation of all of Gemini's rights and defenses. This **RESERVATION OF RIGHTS** extends to all facts, known and unknown, as they might pertain to this claim.

Notice is hereby given by *Redacted* Insurance Company that none of its rights are waived or invalidated, either expressly or by implication, and no commitments are made by this letter, other than as outlined in this letter.

Redacted Insurance Company agrees to a defense of *Redacted* & Associates, Inc. under Policy *Redacted* 1, subject to this **RESERVATION OF RIGHTS** because certain conditions, terms and exclusions contained in Policy *Redacted* issued by *Redacted*. Insurance Company might apply to remove Cross-Complainants claims from the coverage of the Policy *Redacted*, as outlined above. This **RESERVATION OF RIGHTS** is being sent to *Redacted* & Associates, Inc. in order to put you on notice that in the event terms, conditions and/or exclusions contained in Policy *Redacted* operate to remove the claims of the plaintiff from coverage of Policy *Redacted*, then the defense being provided subject to this reservation of rights might be withdrawn by *Redacted* Insurance Company.

More specifically, *Redacted* Insurance Company now takes this opportunity to remind you that the coverage provided under policy *Redacted* is not unlimited. Policy x. provides coverage, subject to the limitations, terms, conditions and exclusions contained in Policy *Redacted*. As a consequence, and because of the nature of the allegations made against *Redacted* & Associates, Inc., there may be a number of reasons why *Redacted* Insurance Company does not have an obligation to provide a defense or indemnify *Redacted* & Associates, Inc. for claims made by the Cross-Complainant in the above-captioned lawsuit, and a number of those reasons are listed above.

Furthermore, *Redacted* Insurance Company specifically does not unilaterally agree to pay any possible verdict or judgment rendered in this case, or agree to indemnify *Redacted* & Associates, Inc. for any possible judgment or verdict rendered in this case, but rather reserves the right to do so. *Redacted* Insurance Company shall have the right to withdraw the defense provided to *Redacted* & Associates, Inc. under Policy *Redacted* subject to this **RESERVATION OF RIGHTS** at any time, and *Redacted* Insurance Company will give *Redacted* & Associates, Inc. written notice of its intent to withdraw.

We have engaged attorney *Redacted* from the *Redacted* law firm to represent the policyholder, *Redacted* & Associates, Inc. Attorney *Redacted* can be reached at *Redacted*. Please give Attorney *Redacted* your full cooperation in the defense of this matter.

Even though *Redacted* Insurance Company chooses to defend this lawsuit filed against *Redacted* & Associates, Inc. under policy *Redacted* subject to this **RESERVATION OF RIGHTS**, *Redacted* Insurance Company specifically reserves the right to assert all defenses of non-coverage available under the terms of Policy *Redacted* Insurance Company does not waive any of its rights under Policy *Redacted* or admit any obligations under Policy *Redacted*.

Any action taken by us in the investigation, defense, or settlement of this claim shall not constitute or be construed as a waiver or an estoppel of any rights or defenses *Redacted* has under the subject policy of insurance. *Redacted* further reserves the right to deny coverage and withdraw from any further participation in this matter altogether, should facts be developed that determine Policy *Redacted* does not cover the loss. Additionally, *Redacted* Insurance Company reserves the right to seek reimbursement from *Redacted* & Associates, Inc. all attorney fees, costs and expenses incurred in connection with this matter if it is subsequently determined that there is no coverage under Policy. *Redacted* further reserves the right to contest coverage available under the subject policy through the filing of a Declaratory Relief Action. The Declaratory Relief Action may be filed in Federal Court or in State Court. As part of the Declaratory Relief Action, *Redacted* Insurance Company may seek to recover from you reimbursement for defense costs and attorneys' fees incurred in providing a defense to *Redacted* & Associates, Inc after the issuance of this reservation of rights letter. Furthermore, *Redacted* Insurance Company specifically reserves the right to seek and to potentially recover attorneys' fees incurred in the Declaratory Relief Action, an action wherein *Redacted* Insurance Company might seek to have a court determine the rights and obligations that *Redacted* Insurance Company has under the subject policy of insurance issued.

Please be advised that *Redacted* Insurance Company will not provide *Redacted* & Associates, Inc. with legal representation or any type of representation for any Declaratory Relief Action, should *Redacted* Insurance Company file a Declaratory Relief Action. *Redacted* & Associates, Inc. will need to select counsel of its own choosing, at its own expense, to protect its interests in any Declaratory Relief Action filed by *Redacted* Insurance Company.

No act of *Redacted* Insurance Company or *Redacted* done by way of said investigation or defense shall be construed as an admission of liability under the subject policies. Likewise, *Redacted* Insurance Company acknowledges and agrees that *Redacted* & Associates, Inc. does not waive or release any of their rights under the subject policy.

In addition to the reservations already made, *Redacted* Insurance Company further reserves the right to assert all defenses of non-coverage available under the subject policies, including all of those specifically listed above, as well as those terms, conditions, exclusions and limitations contained within the subject policies, which might later be determined to be applicable and which might operate to limit or eliminate coverage available under the subject policies. *Redacted* Insurance Company does not waive any of the rights it has under the subject policies, nor does *Redacted* Insurance Company admit any obligations under the subject policies through the issuance of this **RESERVATION OF RIGHTS** letter.

Redacted & Associates has the right to retain your own personal counsel at your own expense, to protect your uninsured interests in the above-captioned lawsuit. Please be advised that in the petition that we have received in the lawsuit, the Cross-Complainants do not allege a specific amount that it is seeking to recover in the lawsuit, nor do the Cross-Complainants designate how much each cross defendant should pay in damages. Consequently, *Redacted* & Associates, Inc. might have a potential uninsured and/or excess exposure above the applicable policy limits. Because the claim involves significant exposure, you might have an uninsured or excess exposure in this case. Consequently, *Redacted* & Associates, Inc. might wish to retain personal counsel, at your own expense, in order to protect your uninsured or excess exposure. *Redacted* Insurance Company will not pay for *Redacted* & Associates, Inc.'s personal attorney.

It may be that *Redacted* & Associates, Inc. has a form of additional coverage that would further extend insurance protection above the limits of the subject policies. If so, your agent or you should report this claim to that carrier accordingly.

If you believe we have overlooked any pertinent facts or anything else in our analysis, or if you feel other reasons might exist regarding coverage potentially available under your subject policies, please advise us as soon as possible, and we will evaluate same. However, in the event any additional information or documentation suggests that the **RESERVATION OF RIGHTS** letter is not complete, *Redacted* Insurance Company specifically reserves the right to amend or to supplement the **RESERVATION OF RIGHTS** letter and assert any and all other coverage defenses as might be warranted.

By naming the specific grounds for the possibility of no coverage or benefits, *Redacted* does not waive any of its rights or any of the other provisions or conditions of the subject policies of insurance, and specifically reserves all of its rights and remedies under the subject policies and under the statutes, case law and common law. *Redacted* **Insurance Company reserves the right to withdraw from the defense of this action and deny indemnification to** *Redacted* **& Associates, Inc. for any judgment rendered.**

In the event you elect to retain independent defense counsel of your own choosing please instruct your defense attorney to maintain accurate and itemized billing records. *Redacted* Insurance Company will only pay those defense fees and costs for work that involve "bodily injury" and "property damage" that occurred during the policy period and that arose from an "occurrence" as defined in the policy *Redacted* Insurance Company reserves the right to require a full accounting from your defense attorney before they will consider making defense cost payments. In the event your defense attorney has any questions in this regard please contact an authorized representative of *Redacted* Insurance Company.

If you have any questions regarding this letter, please do not hesitate to contact me. If you change your address or acquire any information that may affect this coverage analysis, please contact an authorized representative of *Redacted* Insurance Company immediately. If you have any questions regarding the defense of this lawsuit, please do not hesitate to contact your attorney, Mr. *Redacted*. As our investigation continues we may contact you from time to time regarding our need for further information and or documentation related to this claim.

CONSTRUCTION DEFECT CLAIMS/LITIGATION
A Two Case Study

You have the right to have this matter reviewed by the California Department of Insurance, Claims Services Bureau, South Tower, 11th Floor, 300 South Spring Street, Los Angeles, California 90013, or at their telephone number of (213) 897-8921. The California Department of Insurance can also accept complaints over its web site at: www.insurance.ca.gov.

Sincerely yours,

Hugh W. Black CPCU, ARM, AIC, CCLA

(End of Reservation of Rights Sample Letter)

Disclaimer - Information presented in this eBook is for general information purposes only. Any information herein should not be taken as legal advice for any individual case or situation.

www.ingramcontent.com/pod-product-compliance
Lightning Source LLC
Chambersburg PA
CBHW051327220526
45468CB00004B/1529